MW01059679

YOU M' ' THIS

1957

MILESTONES, MEMORIES, TRIVIA AND FACTS, NEWS EVENTS, PROMINENT PERSONALITIES & SPORTS HIGHLIGHTS OF THE YEAR

TO : _____

FROM : _____

MESSAGE : _____

_____

selected and researched
by
mary a. pradt

WARNER 🅦 TREASURES ™

PUBLISHED BY WARNER BOOKS

A TIME WARNER COMPANY

Warner Books, Inc.
1271 Avenue of the Americas
New York, New York 10020

Warner Treasures is a
trademark of Warner Books, Inc.

Ⓦ A Time Warner Company

DESIGN:
CAROL BOKUNIEWICZ DESIGN
PRINTED IN SINGAPORE
FIRST PRINTING : MAY 1995
10 9 8 7 6 5 4 3 2 1
ISBN : 0-446-91033-3

Democratic Senator **john f. kennedy** of Massachusetts, 39, had a high-profile year. A committee JFK headed announced its selection April 30 of five "outstanding senators of the past"; the list included Henry Clay of Kentucky, John C. Calhoun of South Carolina, Daniel Webster of Massachusetts, Robert M. La Follette, Sr., of Wisconsin, and Robert A. Taft of Ohio. On May 6, Senator Kennedy was awarded the Pulitzer Prize for his book *Profiles In Courage.*

AMERICA WAS PROUD OF ITS ACCOMPLISHMENTS IN SCIENCE, TECHNOLOGY, AND SPACE EXPLORATION. ON JULY 16, MAJOR JOHN GLENN, JR., AN OHIO NATIVE, ESTABLISHED A TRANSCONTINENTAL SPEED RECORD, WHEN HE PILOTED A JET FROM CALIFORNIA TO NEW YORK IN THREE HOURS, 23 MINUTES, AND 8.4 SECONDS.

The excitement and paranoia of the Cold War, the Space Race, the Atomic Age, the crisis in race relations, and other themes we indelibly associate with the fifties—all began to coalesce in 1957. A sleepy decade was getting a wakeup call.

newsreel

In the U.S. and worldwide, juvenile delinquency was reaching **"epidemic proportions."** In all the major cities, crimes by young people were escalating. Studies showed that in New York, for example, 50 percent of those arrested for robbery and 60 percent of those accused of burglary were under age 21. In Chicago, L.A., and London (where the miscreants were called **"Teddy boys,"** similar statistics appeared. The upsurge in juvenile crime was attributed to postwar entropy, **"broken homes,"** materialism, the decline in corporal punishment, and even the increase in working moms.

IN AUGUST, THE LONGEST FILIBUSTER TO DATE OCCURRED—SENATOR STROM THURMOND (THEN A DEMOCRAT FROM SOUTH CAROLINA) SPOKE FOR 24 HOURS AND 18 MINUTES, IN OPPOSITION TO THE CIVIL RIGHTS BILL. THURMOND'S AND OTHER SOUTHERN SENATORS' EFFORTS WERE IN VAIN— THE BILL PASSED AUGUST 29. IT WAS THE FIRST MAJOR CIVIL RIGHTS LEGISLATION SINCE RECONSTRUCTION.

nikita khrushchev

consolidated his power in the USSR, after ousting several rivals, including Malenkov and Molotov.

headlines

international

Malaya, the last of Britain's major Asian colonies, gained its independence in August. France's Algerian problem continued. Many Americans, including Senator John F. Kennedy, favored Algerian independence. In Africa, the former British Togoland and the Gold Coast united to form independent Ghana, with Kwame Nkrumah as its first head.

The International Geophysical Year began July 1.

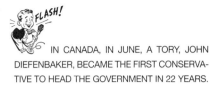

IN CANADA, IN JUNE, A TORY, JOHN DIEFENBAKER, BECAME THE FIRST CONSERVATIVE TO HEAD THE GOVERNMENT IN 22 YEARS.

THE TREATY ESTABLISHING A EUROPEAN COMMON MARKET WAS SIGNED IN ROME MARCH 25.

sputnik I,
the world's first earth-orbiting artificial satellite, was launched by the USSR October 4. In November, a second satellite was launched, this one carrying a dog named Laika.

5

the beat generation

began, described by Jack Kerouac's depiction in
On the Road. Coffeehouses, poetry readings, and
antimaterialist values characterized the Beats.

IN JULY, REVEREND BILLY GRAHAM DREW 100,000, A RECORD CROWD, TO YANKEE STADIUM. HIS 1957 CRUSADE CAUSED THOUSANDS TO MAKE "DECISIONS FOR CHRIST," AND MANY MORE TO BE "SAVED" FOLLOWING IT ON TV.

In December, Macy's recorded the first $2 million shopping day in history.

the flying disc, or **frisbee,** took hold as an enduring fad. It was first popular on college campuses.

cultural
milestones

Even as rock and roll was taking hold, Pat Boone, a married straight-A student with two children, presented a more wholesome image. His white bucks and good manners contrasted with the Elvis trend and appealed to many. Bruce Dern, a track star at the Universty of Pennsylvania, resigned from the team rather than shave his Elvis-style sideburns.

Queen Elizabeth II made her first visit to America as sovereign in October, to celebrate the 350th anniversary of Jamestown. A million spectators turned out in Washington to glimpse her.

television

top-rated tv series of the fall 1957 season :

1. "Gunsmoke" (CBS)

2. "The Danny Thomas Show" (CBS)

3. "Tales of Wells Fargo" (NBC)

4. "Have Gun, Will Travel" (CBS)

5. "I've Got a Secret" (CBS)

6. "The Life and Legend of Wyatt Earp" (ABC)

7. "General Electric Theater" (CBS)

8. "The Restless Gun" (NBC)

9. "December Bride" (CBS)

10. "You Bet Your Life"—Groucho Marx (NBC)

11. "The Perry Como Show" (NBC)

12. "Alfred Hitchcock Presents" (CBS)

13. "Cheyenne" (ABC)

14. "The Ford Show" (NBC)

15. "The Red Skelton Show" (CBS)

16. "The Gale Storm Show" (CBS)

17. "The Millionaire" (CBS)

18. "The Lineup" (CBS)

19. "This Is Your Life" (NBC)

20. "The $64,000 Question" (CBS)

Yankee baseball great **DON LARSEN,** 28, who pitched the only perfect game in World Series history, married former flight attendant **CORRINE AUDREY BRUESS,** 26, in December.

celeb wedding of the year
milestones

HARRY LILLIS (BING) CROSBY, multimillionaire crooner, golfer, and horseman, 53, married actress **KATHY GRANT,** 23. His first wife, Dixie Lee, mother of the first four Crosby sons, had died in 1952.

MARLON BRANDO, 33, married actress **ANNA KASHFI (JOHANNA O'CALLAGHAN),** 23, in California in October.

STIRLING MOSS, English auto-racing star, 28, married **KATHERINE MOLSON,** brewery heiress, 22, in London in October.

10

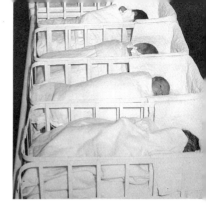

D E A T H S

Joseph McCarthy,
senator whose name was linked with rabid anticommunism and who was censured for his extreme tactics, died May 2 of liver disease.

Arturo Toscanini,
regarded as the foremost conductor of the age, died January 16 at 89.

Laura Ingalls Wilder,
who wrote the Little House series for children, died at 90 on February 10.

Jimmy Dorsey,
bandleader, died on June 12. His brother Tommy had died in November 1956.

Edna Woolman Chase,
Vogue editor and Legion of Honor winner, died March 20.

The Aga Khan III,
spiritual and temporal leader of many Muslims worldwide, died July 11.

Clarence Birdseye,
inventor of frozen foods, died October 7.

Humphrey Bogart,
screen legend, died January 14 of throat cancer at 57. He was survived by his wife, Lauren Bacall.

Admiral Richard Byrd,
U.S. explorer, passed away in March.

Louis B. Mayer,
film producer, died October 29.

Christian Dior,
the dean of Paris couture, died in Italy on October 24 at 52.

Sir Richard Oppenheimer,
one of the world's richest men and boss of the DeBeers diamond cartel, died in November at 77.

births

CAROLINE, Princess of Monaco, was born January 23.

CAROLINE BOUVIER KENNEDY, daughter of John F. Kennedy, 40, and Jacqueline Lee Bouvier Kennedy, 28, was born November 27.

VANNA WHITE, TV personality, was born February 18.

GEENA DAVIS was born January 21.

BILL LAIMBEER, basketball player, was born May 19.

SEVE BALLESTEROS, golfer, was born April 9.

ALBERTO SALAZAR, running great, was born August 7.

BRETT BUTLER, baseball player, was born June 15.

JON LOVITZ, comedian, was born July 21.

NANCY LOPEZ, golfer, was born January 6.

DANIEL DAY-LEWIS, actor, was born April 29.

MARLON JACKSON, of Jackson 5 fame, was born March 12.

EDDIE VAN HALEN, musician, was born in the Netherlands January 26.

'57

1. **all shook up** Elvis Presley
2. **love letters in the sand** Pat Boone
3. **jailhouse rock** Elvis Presley
4. **(let me be your) teddy bear** Elvis Presley
5. **april love** Pat Boone
6. **young love** Tab Hunter
7. **tammy** Debbie Reynolds
8. **honeycomb** Jimmie Rodgers

hit music

9. **wake up little susie** Everly Brothers
10. **you send me** Sam Cooke
11. **butterfly** Andy Williams
12. **too much** Elvis Presley
13. **round and round** Perry Como
14. **butterfly** Charlie Gracie
15. **chances are** Johnny Mathis
16. **young love** Sonny James
17. **diana** Paul Anka
18. **don't forbid me** Pat Boone
19. **party doll** Buddy Knox
20. **that'll be the day** Crickets

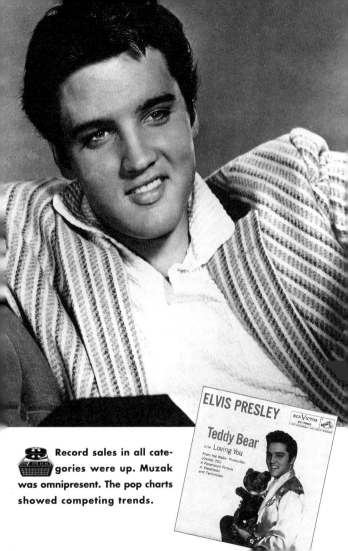

Record sales in all cate-gories were up. Muzak was omnipresent. The pop charts showed competing trends.

bestselling

fiction

1. **by love possessed**
   james gould cozzens

2. **peyton place**
   grace metalious

3. **compulsion**
   meyer levin

4. **rally round the flag, boys!**
   max shulman

5. **blue camellia**
   frances parkinson keyes

6. **eloise in paris**
   kay thompson

7. **the scapegoat**
   daphne duMaurier

8. **on the beach**
   nevil shute

9. **below the salt**
   thomas b. costain

10. **atlas shrugged**
    ayn rand

books

BOXING

Carmen Basilio was the man of the year, winning a split decision over Sugar Ray Robinson at Yankee Stadium on September 23. Heavyweight Floyd Patterson had two opponents in 1957, but neither was a serious challenge.

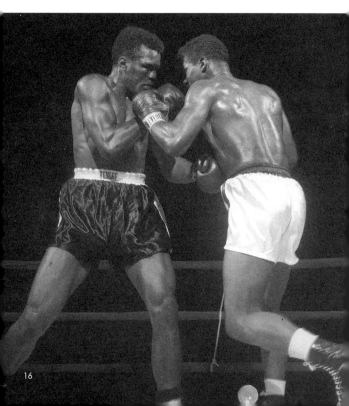

The Montreal Canadiens won the 1957 Stanley Cup for the second season in a row. It was their eighth cup championship.

THE ACHIEVEMENTS OF BLACK ATHLETE ALTHEA GIBSON ENHANCED U.S. PRESTIGE IN THE SPORT. GIBSON BECAME THE FIRST BLACK TO WIN AT WIMBLEDON, AND SHE ALSO TOOK THE LAURELS AT FOREST HILLS.

THE OKLAHOMA SOONERS EXTENDED THEIR WINNING STREAK TO 47 GAMES BUT WERE DEFEATED BY THE FIGHTING IRISH OF NOTRE DAME NOVEMBER 16.

sports

IN BASEBALL, the Milwaukee Braves, a major-league team for only five years, won the National League pennant and then went on to beat the vaunted New York Yankees in the World Series, 4 games to 3. Series hero was pitcher Lew Burdette. The Series set a 7-game attendance record. Ticket sales, at $2,475,978, also set a record for receipts. The major-league batting title went to the Boston Red Sox's Ted Williams, at 39 the oldest man to earn it.

top
box-office
stars

Rock Hudson
•
John Wayne
•
Pat Boone
•
Elvis Presley
•
Frank Sinatra
•
Gary Cooper
•
William Holden
•
James Stewart
•
Jerry Lewis
•
Yul Brynner

Oscars went to ***The Bridge on the River Kwai*** and its star **Alec Guinness.** The film also took directing honors for **David Lean,** and cinematography and film editing Oscars. **Joanne Woodward** won Best Actress honors for her multifaceted portrayal of ***The Three Faces of Eve,*** America's first exposure to multiple personality disorder. Woodward beat out some stiff competition— Anna Magnani, Deborah Kerr, Elizabeth Taylor, and Lana Turner. Best Supporting Actor and Actress awards went to **Red Buttons** and **Miyoshi Umeki,** both for their roles in ***Sayonara.***

box-office champs

1. **The Ten Commandments** ($ 18,500,000)
2. **Around the World in 80 Days** ($16,200,000)
3. **Giant** ($12,000,000)
4. **Pal Joey** ($6,700,000)
5. **Seven Wonders of the World** ($6,500,000)
6. **Teahouse of the August Moon** ($5,600,000)
7. **The Pride and the Passion** ($5,500,000)
8. **Anastasia** ($5,000,000)
9. **Island in the Sun** ($5,000,000)
10. **Love Me Tender** ($4,500,000)

OTHER FILMS THAT GROSSED OVER $3,500,00 INCLUDED: WRITTEN ON THE WIND, GUNFIGHT AT THE OK CORRAL, HEAVEN KNOWS, MR. ALLISON, APRIL LOVE, JAILHOUSE ROCK, BATTLE HYMN, AN AFFAIR TO REMEMBER, BERNADINE, LOVING YOU, AND THE SUN ALSO RISES.

movies

Average weekly attendance was 45,000,000, and the average admission price was 50.5 cents. There were 19,000 movie houses in the U.S.

'57

The trend to compact cars was just starting to take off.

It was a comeback year for Chrysler as a result of its styling innovations. More model changes were designed for 1957 than for any previous year. High tailfins were the favorite feature, especially for Chrysler. Ford Motor Company extended the fins

cars

upward and curved them outward as well. Other styling features included larger, wraparound windshields, 14-inch wheels, retractable backlights and more use of decorative anodized aluminum.

 One major high-light was the phenomenal rise in populari-ty of imported cars. Foreign-car sales started to take off at the end of 1954, almost doubled in 1955 and again in 1956. VW led the way in imports, followed by the French-built Renault. Toyota of Japan announced plans to bring an $1,100 compact car to the U.S. market.

IN 1957 **FORD** ANNOUNCED SOME-THING COMPLETELY DIFFERENT IN CARS— THE SOON-TO-BE INFA-MOUS **EDSEL**, WHICH WAS ONE OF THE ALL-TIME GREATEST BOMBS IN THE AUTO INDUSTRY.

Necklines and backlines plunged daringly.

fashion

Some of the fashion statements that emerged in 1957 now seem misguided and dated—notably the **"sack"** silhouette. This shape was like a giant almond with sleeves, tapering to a narrow hem that reached just below the kneecap. Some designers combined the sack and the sheath, by veiling a form-fitting dress with a loose, straight overdress of transparent fabric. Others played with **"modernistic"** shapes, variously called **"egg," "melon,"** and **"balloon"** skirts.

Many designers designed from head to toe; they created hats, shoes, jewelry, and even hosiery to coordinate with their garments.

Necklines and backlines plunged daringly. The underwear industry had to design backless, frontless, and strapless bras to, er, keep up. Pointy-toed patent leather shoes with medium heels were the norm.

in menswear,

pastel colors were coming on strong. Pink jackets, dinner clothes, and shirts were popular for town and country. A leisure jacket for at-home wear was essential. In suits, charcoal gray and brown were giving way to checks and tweeds. Ascots were a popular affectation. Paisley ties and handkerchiefs were in.

final

factoid

A man named Geisel who called himself

dr. seuss

pushed and pushed until he succeeded in getting his work published; *The Cat in the Hat* remains popular to this day, as do many of his other works.

THE CAT
IN
THE
HAT

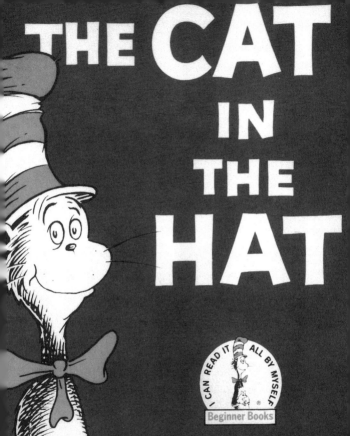

I CAN READ IT ALL BY MYSELF
Beginner Books

By Dr. Seuss

credits

archive photos: pages 1, 5, 6, 7, 10, 11, 15, 20, 21, 22, inside back cover.

associated press: pages 4, 16.

photofest: inside front cover, pages 2, 8, 9, 12, 13, 18, 19.

original photography:
beth phillips: pages 13, 25.

album cover:
courtesy of bob george/
the archive of contemporary music: page 13

photo research:
alice albert

coordination:
rustyn birch

design:
carol bokuniewicz design
mutsumi hyuga

'57